English for Mathematics

Karen Greenway

Series Editor: Mary Wood

William Collins' dream of knowledge for all began with the publication of his first book in 1819.
A self-educated mill worker, he not only enriched millions of lives, but also founded a flourishing publishing house.
Today, staying true to this spirit, Collins books are packed with inspiration, innovation and practical expertise.
They place you at the centre of a world of possibility and give you exactly what you need to explore it.

Collins. Freedom to teach

HarperCollins*Publishers*
The News Building
1 London Bridge Street
London SE1 9GF

**Browse the complete Collins catalogue at
www.collins.co.uk**

First edition 2015

10 9 8 7 6 5 4 3 2 1

© HarperCollins*Publishers* 2015

ISBN 978-0-00-813570-6

Collins® is a registered trademark of HarperCollins Publishers Limited

www.collins.co.uk

A catalogue record for this book is available from the British Library

Written by Karen Greenway
Series edited by Mary Wood
Commissioned and conceptualised by Karen Jamieson
Editorial management by Mike Appleton
Copyedited by Tasia Vassilatou
Proofread by Cassie Fox
Artwork and typesetting by QBS
Cover design by Amparo Barrera and Ken Vail Graphic Design
Printed and bound by CPI Group (UK) Ltd, Croydon

Introduction

This series of books is aimed at non-native English speakers who attend English language mathematics lessons in primary school. The books aim to support those who find the language used in the lesson unfamiliar and challenging.

Some of the language of mathematics is rarely used outside the classroom, so may be unfamiliar to those students who don't speak English as their first language. In some cases words and phrases can have a different meaning in the mathematics classroom to their meaning in common usage. This can lead to confusion and frustration, and can hinder progress.

The *English for Mathematics* series aims to teach students the language used for mathematics taught in upper primary school. Key words and language structures are explained, using diagrams and illustrations to aid understanding. The 'Wise Owl' gives tips and hints on how to use the language, allowing learners to check their understanding. Carefully graded activities linked to the topic and the focus vocabulary give opportunities to practise using the language.

Each of the 36 units includes notes to teachers or parents, which give ideas for how to present the language and topics to learners. The books can be used in class alongside the main textbook, or at home for further practice and reinforcement.

The clear, easy-to-use layout, and the appealing and helpful pictures and diagrams, will help de-mystify the English of Mathematics.

Mary Wood, Series Editor

English for Mathematics: Book A
Karen Greenway

Contents

Number

1. Read and write numbers to 1000 6
2. Partition numbers 8
3. Order and compare numbers 10
4. Patterns and sequences 12
5. Rounding 14
6. Fractions 16
7. Equivalent fractions 18
8. Mixed numbers 20
9. Addition 22
10. Subtraction 24
11. Addition and subtraction facts 26
12. Multiplication 28
13. Division 30
14. Doubles and halves 32
15. Times tables 34
16. Word problems 36

Geometry

17. 2D shapes 38
18. Regular shapes 40
19. Right angles 42
20. Line symmetry 44
21. 3D shapes 46
22. Pyramids and prisms 48
23. Nets 50
24. Position and movement 52
25. Using grids 54

Measures

26. Length 56
27. Mass 58
28. Capacity 60
29. Telling the time 62
30. Using a calendar 64
31. Using measurements 66

Data handling

32. Tally charts 68
33. Bar charts 70
34. Pictograms 72
35. Carroll diagrams 74
36. Venn diagrams 76

Key words 78

Read and write numbers to 1000

Read it!

Key words: digit, place of, place value, unit, ten, hundred, thousand

The **digits** 0, 1, 2, 3, 4, 5, 6, 7, 8 and 9 are used to write all numbers.
The position of a **digit** in a number gives its **place value**.

hundreds   tens   units

H	T	U
8	2	9

Example:
Question: Write the number 546 in words.
Answer: five hundred and forty-six

We write questions about **place value** in different ways.

H	T	U
7	1	8

Question: Which digit is in the tens place?
Answer: 1
Question: What is the value of the 7 in this number?
Answer: seven hundreds (or 700)

Language focus!
Units/Multiples of 10

two/twenty, three/thirty, four/forty,
five/fifty, six/sixty, seven/seventy,
eight/eighty, nine/ninety

The number after

H	T	U
9	9	9

is

thousands

Th	H	T	U
1	0	0	0

This is called one **thousand**.

Think about it!

1. **Write nine hundred and twenty-three in digits.**

   _____

2. **Write 472 in words.**

   _____

3. **What is the value of the 5 in 953?**

   _____

Practise it!

1. Write the 6 in the tens place.

   Write the 3 in the units place.

   Write the 1 in the hundreds place.

   Write the whole number in words. _____

2. | 7 | 0 | 9 | (a) What is the value of the 7 in this number? _____

   (b) Which digit is in the units place? _____

3. **Benny has 3 digit cards.**

   He places them on this diagram to make different 3-digit numbers.

   (a) Write the largest number he makes in words.   _____

   _____

   (b) Write the smallest number he makes in digits.   _____

   _____

   (c) List all of the other numbers that he makes.   _____

   _____

Teachers' and parents' note

Encourage students to use a place value diagram and
digit cards to make, read and write different numbers.

Discuss the use of zero in the number 502 as a place holder – there are no tens but we cannot
leave the column blank as the number would become 52.

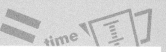

Partition numbers

Read it!

Key words: partition, hundreds, tens, units

Numbers are split into **hundreds**, **tens** and **units** to make them easier to use in calculations. This is called **partitioning**.

H	T	U
3	7	2

= 3 hundreds + 7 tens + 2 units
= 300 + 70 + 2

Example:
Question: Partition 694.
Answer: 6 hundreds + 9 tens + 4 units or
600 + 90 + 4

Language focus!
Focus words

Everyday meaning of **partition**: a screen dividing a room into parts

Mathematical meaning of **partition**: split a number into parts, for example 27 = 20 + 7

Zero is used as a place holder.

The number nine hundred and five is written as 905.

Without the zero holding the tens place the number would be ninety-five written as 95.

H	T	U
9	0	5

place holder

Think about it!

Write a digit in each box to make the partitioning correct.

1. 836 = ☐ hundreds + 3 tens + ☐ units

2. 2☐7 = 2 hundreds + 4 tens + ☐ units

3. 59☐ = ☐ hundreds + 9 tens + 8 units

Practise it!

1. Partition these numbers.

Example: $475 = 400 + 70 + 5$

(a) 143 _____

(b) 609 _____

(c) 827 _____

Numbers are partitioned in different ways to help in different calculations.

325 is   3 hundreds + 2 tens + 5 units

or 3 hundreds + 1 ten + 15 units

or 2 hundreds + 12 tens + 5 units

2. Gustav partitions the number 536.

Here are his answers.

$500 + 30 + 6$

$400 + 120 + 6$

$500 + 20 + 16$

$400 + 110 + 26$

$500 + 10 + 16$

Tick all the correct answers.

3. Partition 269 in four different ways.

_____

_____

_____

_____

Order and compare numbers

Read it!

Key words: compare, in between, greater than, largest, less than, order, smallest

Numbers on a number line are **in order**.

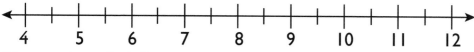

The numbers 5, 6, 7 and 8 are **in between** 4 and 9.

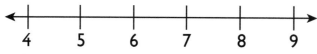

A list of numbers is put in **order** from **smallest** to **largest**.

23, 27, 35, 52, 73, 75

or from **largest** to **smallest**

399, 359, 319, 279, 239

Example:
Question: Which numbers are in between 21 and 25?
Answer: 22, 23 and 24

The symbols < and > are used to **compare** numbers.

>
means
greater than
100 > 95

<
means
less than
47 < 50

Language focus!
Opposites

>	<
greater than	less than
larger than	smaller than
more than	less than
higher than	lower than

If the numbers are the same, use the equals (=) sign.

Think about it!

1. **Put these numbers in order from smallest to largest.**

   30, 16, 3, 6, 23, 20

   _____

2. **Put these numbers in order from largest to smallest.**

   205, 125, 250, 152, 175

   _____

Practise it!

1. **Write a whole number that is in between:**

   (a) 12 and 15 _____   (b) 64 and 69 _____

   (c) 138 and 142 _____   (d) 599 and 605 _____

2. **Write > or < in each circle to make these statements correct.**

   (a) 19 ◯ 26   (b) 55 ◯ 51

   (c) 210 ◯ 208

   (d) 391 ◯ 400

3. **Draw a line to join each number to the correct place on the number line.**

   | 235 | | 207 | | 299 | | 261 |

   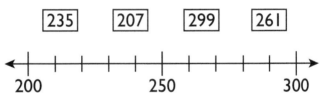

   200   250   300

Teachers' and parents' note

Give students experience of ordering numbers using number cards or on blank number lines.

Using an image such as the open mouth of a greedy crocodile (or other appropriate animal) may help students remember that > means 'greater than' and < means 'less than', as the crocodile always eats the larger number.

Patterns and sequences

Read it!

Key words: count on, count back, continue, pattern, rule, sequence

A **pattern** is a repeating set of objects such as shapes or numbers.

This pattern **continues** by repeating.

In a **sequence** the numbers follow a **rule**.

In this sequence

1, 3, 5, 7, 9 …

the rule is **count on** (⌒) in twos.

Example:

Question: What is the next number in this pattern?

2   2   3   3   2   2   3   3

Answer: 2

Count on (⌒) in tens.

123, 133, 143, 153 …

Count back (⌒) in ones.

97, 96, 95, 94 …

Language focus!

Everyday meaning of **pattern**: a template for making clothes or a design on wallpaper or fabric

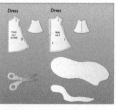

Mathematical meaning of **pattern**: a repeating set of shapes or numbers

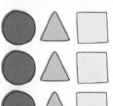

We can count on and back to help us remember larger numbers and to describe sequences.

6

Think about it!

Here is a number sequence: 5, 10, 15, 20 ...
The rule is: count on in fives.

Write the next three numbers in the sequence.

5, 10, 15, 20, _____, _____, _____

Practise it!

1. **Write the next three numbers in these sequences.**

    (a) Count on in hundreds.

    150, 250, 350, _____, _____, _____

    (b) Count back in tens.

    142, 132, 122, 112, _____, _____, _____

    (c) Count on in threes.

    1, 4, 7, 10, _____, _____, _____,

2. **Colour the blank shapes to continue these patterns.**

    (a)

    (b)

    (c)

3. **Here is a number sequence: 22, 24, 26, 28 ...**

    (a) What is the next number in the sequence? _____

    (b) What rule did you use to continue the sequence? _____

Teachers' and parents' note

Use sets of objects such as counters and shapes to make and extend patterns.
Encourage students to count out loud in ones, tens and hundreds to develop larger numbers and sequences.

Rounding

Read it!

Key words: round, round down, round up, round to the nearest

A number is **rounded to the nearest** 10 or 100 when an accurate answer is not needed.

Example:

Question: How many children were in the concert?

Answer: About 10.

This number line shows how to **round to the nearest** 10.

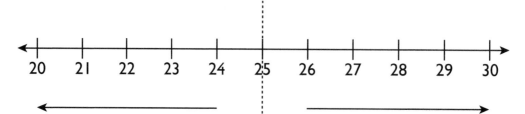

| 20 21 22 23 24 25 26 27 28 29 30 |

Round down if the number is **less than** half way to the next ten so 24, 23, 22 and 21 round to 20.

Round up if the number is **more than** half way to the next ten so 26, 27, 28 and 29 round to 30.

25 is exactly half way to 30 this number always **rounds up**

Example:

Question: Round 32 to the nearest 10.

Answer: 30

Language focus!

Focus words

Everyday meaning of **round**: something that is circular – a circle or plate is round

Mathematical meaning of **round**: take a number to the nearest 10 or 100

When rounding to 100, the number 50 is half way. Numbers that are less than 50 **round down** and numbers that are more than 50 round up. The number 50 also **rounds up**.

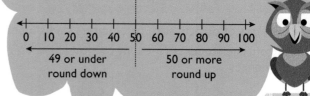

0 10 20 30 40 50 60 70 80 90 100

49 or under round down

50 or more round up

Think about it!

1. **Round these numbers to the nearest 10.**

   (a) 17 _____ (b) 45 _____ (c) 63 _____

2. **Round these numbers to the nearest 100.**

   (a) 150 _____ (b) 594 _____ (c) 325 _____

Practise it!

1. **Fill in the circle and rectangle. Round each number ...**

   (a) in the circle to the nearest 10.

   (b) in the rectangle to the nearest 100.

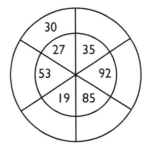

2. **Round the number of people at each event to the nearest 100.**

   (a) concert: 475 people _____

   (b) museum: 234 people _____

   (c) sports event: 750 people _____

3. **The table below shows the fruit sold by a shop on one day.**

   Round each number to the nearest 10.

Fruit	Number sold	Round to nearest 10
apples	83	
bananas	60	
melons	18	
oranges	45	

Teachers' and parents' note

Discuss situations where rounding is used in real life, for example the number of people at an event (about 500), the cost of an item (about $10), the time taken to get somewhere (about half an hour).

Show how rounding can be used in calculations. For example: $17 + 9$, where 9 is nearly 10, so $17 + 10 = 27$ and then one less.

Fractions

Read it!

Key words: fraction, equal part, half, third, quarter, whole

A **fraction** is any part of a whole, a group or a number.

A fraction of a whole:

A square is split into two equal parts. Each part is **half** of the square.

$\frac{1}{2}$ ☐ $\frac{2}{2}$ ☐   1

A half is a **fraction**.
We write one half as $\frac{1}{2}$. Two halves is $\frac{2}{2}$ or 1 **whole**.

A fraction of a group:

3 students share 12 cherries equally between them.
Each student has one third ($\frac{1}{3}$) of the cherries.

One third of 12 is 4.
This can be written as $\frac{1}{3}$ of 12 = 4

This pizza is divided into 2 equal parts. Each part is half of the pizza.

This pizza is divided into 4 equal parts. Each part is one quarter of the pizza.

Language focus!

Singular	Plural
half	halves
quarter	quarters
third	thirds

If you eat **two quarters** ($\frac{2}{4}$) of the pizza, this is the same as **a half** ($\frac{1}{2}$). Look at the pizza picture.

Think about it!

Put a tick (✓) next to the diagrams with one quarter shaded in.

Practise it!

1. **Here are four squares divided into parts.**

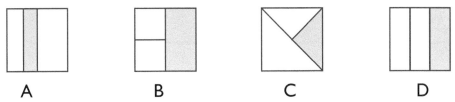

| A | B | C | D |

Which square has $\frac{1}{3}$ shaded? Write A, B, C or D. _____

2. There are 16 cubes on a table.

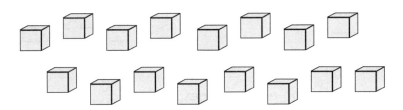

   (a) Draw lines on the diagram to show how the cubes can be divided into four equal parts.

   (b) Hassan uses three quarters of the cubes to make a model. How many cubes does he use? _____

   (c) How many cubes does Hassan have left? _____

   (d) What fraction of the 16 cubes does Hassan have left? _____

3. Fatima decorates $\frac{2}{3}$ of these tiles.

   (a) How many tiles does Fatima decorate? _____

   (b) What fraction of the tiles are not decorated? _____

Teachers' and parents' note

Discuss how we use fractions in everyday life, for example by asking: 'Please cut the cake into quarters' or 'What fraction of the glass is filled with water?' Emphasise that these fractions are unlikely to be exact. You might hear someone say: 'I want the bigger half!' In mathematics, two halves, three thirds and four quarters must be exactly the same size, so 'having a bigger half' is mathematically impossible.

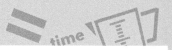

Equivalent fractions

Read it!

Equivalent means 'of equal value'. **Equivalent** fractions may look different.

A **half** is **equivalent** to two **quarters** or four **eighths**.

$$\frac{1}{2} = \frac{2}{4} = \frac{4}{8}$$

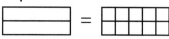

Example:

Question: How many tenths are equivalent to a half?

Answer: 5 tenths

We can also show equivalence using number lines.

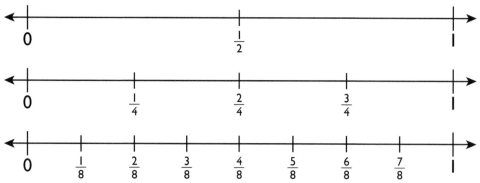

Language focus!

We talk about **equivalent** fractions, not **equal** fractions because the fractions may look different.

We use an equals sign to show **equivalence.**

$$\frac{1}{2} = \frac{2}{4}$$

One half is equivalent to two quarters.

The shaded parts of a fraction diagram can be arranged in different ways. They must cover the same amount of space. These diagrams show six different ways of showing two quarters.

Think about it!

Put a tick (✓) by in the diagrams where the equivalent of a half is shaded.

Practise it!

1. Shade $\frac{1}{2}$ of each shape.

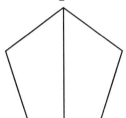 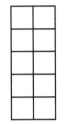 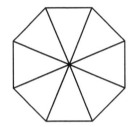 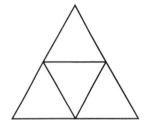

2. Colour half of these flags yellow.

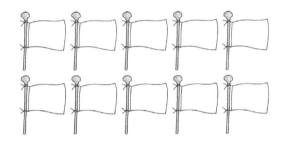

Complete these number sentences.

(a) $\frac{1}{2}$ of $\boxed{}$ = 5

(b) $\frac{1}{2} = \dfrac{\boxed{}}{10}$

3. Here are three digits: 1   2   4

Use each digit once to make this statement correct.

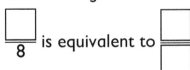

$\dfrac{\boxed{}}{8}$ is equivalent to $\dfrac{\boxed{}}{\boxed{}}$

Teachers' and parents' note

Ask students to find different ways of dividing a 4 × 2 rectangle in half. For example:

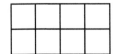 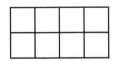 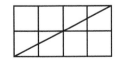

$$\frac{1}{2} = \frac{4}{8}$$

Mixed numbers

Read it!

Key word: mixed number

A **mixed number** is a whole number and a fraction.

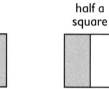

This is written as $1\frac{1}{2}$

This is $2\frac{1}{4}$ as a **mixed number**.

Example:

Question: Which mixed number is shown by this diagram?

Answer: $5\frac{1}{2}$

Language focus!

Singular	Plural
half	halves
quarter	quarters
eighth	eighths
tenth	tenths

Mixed numbers can also be shown on number lines like these.

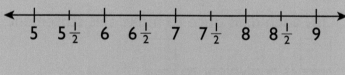

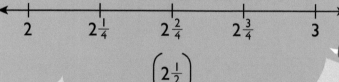

$\left(2\frac{1}{2}\right)$

Think about it!

Write a mixed number in each box to complete the number lines.

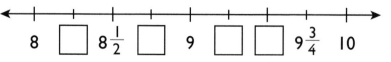

8 ☐ $8\frac{1}{2}$ ☐ 9 ☐ ☐ $9\frac{3}{4}$ 10

Practise it!

1. Draw a line to match each diagram to the correct mixed number.

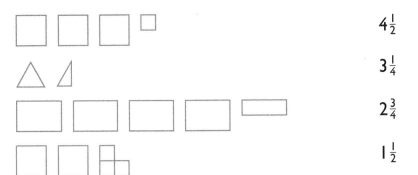

$4\frac{1}{2}$

$3\frac{1}{4}$

$2\frac{3}{4}$

$1\frac{1}{2}$

2. Draw diagrams on the grid to show these mixed numbers.

(a) $1\frac{1}{4}$

(b) $3\frac{1}{2}$

(c) $2\frac{3}{4}$

3. Draw a line to match each mixed number to the correct place on the number line.

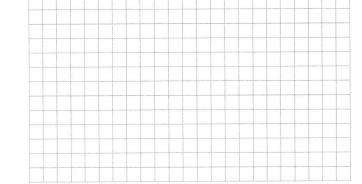

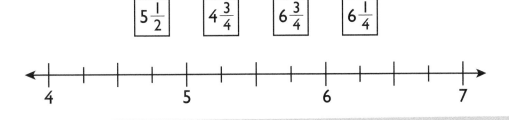

Teachers' and parents' note

Ask students to count on and back in halves or quarters from a given number to practise using mixed numbers. Give students practical experience of writing mixed numbers on number lines.

Addition

Read it!

Addition joins one or **more** numbers to give a **total** or **sum**. The symbol for **addition** is +. Changing the order of the numbers in the addition does not change the answer.

An equals sign (=) shows the answer.

Example:

Question: Add 15 and 32.

Answer: $15 + 32 = 47$

equals sign

$2 + 8 = 10$

addition sign   total

Language focus!

Addition words

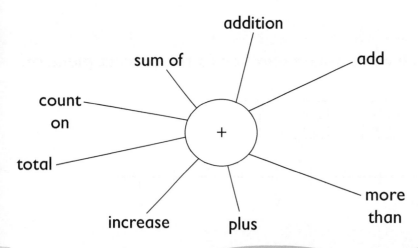

Use jottings like these to help you add larger numbers.

Add numbers by partitioning.

$23 + 59$
$20 + 50 = 70$
$3 + 9 = 12$
$70 + 12 = 82$

Count on using a number line.

+10   +10   +3

59   69   79 82

Think about it!

1. What is the sum of 34 and 25?

_____

2. What is 49 more than 18?

_____

3. Find the total of 135 and 63.

_____

Practise it!

1. Write a number that is 70 more than:

   (a) 108 _____   (b) 235 _____   (c) 561 _____

2. Increase these numbers by 300. Write the numbers.

   (a) 17 _____   (b) 138 _____   (c) 403 _____

3. Solve these word problems.

   (a) How many pencils are there altogether?

   _____ pencils

22 pencils   36 pencils

   (b) A teacher has 125 counters.

   She finds 65 more.

   What is the total number of counters?

   _____ counters

   (c) What is 53 plus 66?

   _____

Teachers' and parents' note

Encourage students to use all the different vocabulary for addition by using appropriate real life situations. Ask them to count on 12 beads or increase the number of pencils in a box by 7.

Make sure that they understand that the only meaning of 'sum' is 'addition'; explain 'sum' is often misused to mean any type of calculation.

Subtraction

Read it!

Key words: count back, decrease by, difference between, leave, less than, minus, subtract, take away

Subtraction is finding the **difference between** two numbers.
One number is **taken away** from another.
The symbol for **subtraction** is −

Example:
Question: Take 23 from 79
Answer: $79 - 23 = 56$

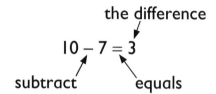

the difference

$$10 - 7 = 3$$

subtract   equals

Use jottings to help you subtract larger numbers.

Subtract by partitioning.
$76 - 23$
$70 - 20 = 50$
$6 - 3 = 3$
$76 - 23 = 53$

Count back on a number line.

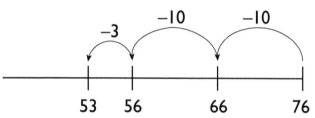

-10 -10

-3

53   56   66   76

Language focus!
Subtraction words

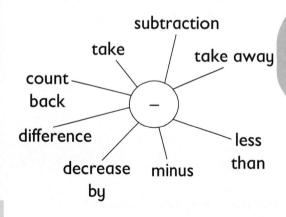

subtraction

take   take away

count back

−

difference

less than

decrease by   minus

Beware of the word **difference**.
Its meaning changes in everyday situations.

Mathematical meaning	Everyday meaning
$8 - 7 = 1$	8 has curved lines 7 has straight lines

Think about it!

1. Subtract 16 from 49.   **2. Take 76 away from 158.**

_____   _____

Practise it!

1. Write the number that is 40 less than:

(a) 95 _____   (b) 137 _____   (c) 309 _____

2. Decrease these numbers by 200.

(a) 315 _____   (b) 572 _____   (c) 804 _____

3. Solve these word problems.

(a) What is the difference between the number of fish in these fish tanks?

_____ fish

8 fish   12 fish

(b) Pete and Izaak collect stickers.

Pete has 72 stickers.

Izaak has 25 fewer.

How many stickers does Izaak have?

_____ stickers

(c) What is 179 minus 87? _____

(d) A plane flying from Paris to Beijing has 376 passenger seats.

289 passengers are on the plane.

How many empty seats are there? _____

Teachers' and parents' note

Discuss the use of 'more than' and 'less than' as they can be used in ways that could mislead students.

For example: Hassan has 18 tokens. That is 7 more than he had last week. How many tokens did he have last week? The word 'more' usually suggests 'add' so many students would answer '25'. However, in this case we need to use the inverse, as the problem works backwards – the answer is 11.

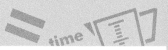

Addition and subtraction facts

Read it!

Key words: answer, equals, missing number, number sentence, operation, represents

A **number sentence** is how a calculation is written.
It uses an **operation** such as addition (+) or subtraction (−) and an **equals** sign (=) to show the **answer**.

Example:
Question: What is twenty minus six?
Answer: $20 - 6 = 14$

equals

$9 + 11 = 20$

operation   answer

Sometimes, instead of the **answer**, one of the **numbers** or the **operation** is **missing**. A symbol such as a square or circle is used to **represent** this.

$35 + \square = 100$ $100 \bigcirc 15 = 85$

$\square$ represents 65 $\bigcirc$ represents −

Language focus!
Opposites

add	subtract
more	less
increase	decrease
count on	count back

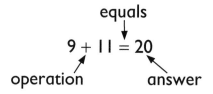

Look for pairs of numbers that total 10 to help add several small numbers.

10

$3 + 6 + 5 + 7 + 4 =$

10

$10 + 10 + 5 = 25$

Think about it!

Write a number in each box to make the calculations correct.

$15 + \boxed{} = 20$ $\qquad$ $20 - \boxed{} = 12$ $\qquad$ $\boxed{} - 6 = 14$

Practise it!

1. Here is a 3 digit number.

$\boxed{490}$

(a) Write the number that is 100 more than this number? _____

(b) Write the number that is 1 less than this number. _____

(c) Increase the number by 10. Write the new number. _____

2. Write + or − in each circle to make these calculations correct.

(a) $63 \bigcirc 20 = 43$ $\qquad$ (b) $172 \bigcirc 50 = 222$

(c) $349 \bigcirc 400 = 749$ $\qquad$ (d) $596 \bigcirc 70 = 526$

3. Solve these word problems.

Write a complete number sentence to show your answer.

For example: $19 + 20 = 39$

(a) Sophia has 2 red beads, 4 blue beads, 8 yellow beads, 7 green beads and 6 black beads.

How many beads does she have altogether? _____

(b) There are 100 pins in a packet.

Benji uses 38 pins.

How many pins are left in the packet? _____

(c) Nouma has 55 star stickers.

How many more does she need to make 100? _____

Teachers' and parents' note

Encourage students to use a variety of mental strategies such as addition facts to 10 or 20 or multiples of 5 that total 100 to aid their calculations.

Multiplication

Read it!

Key words: **array, columns, group, groups of, lots of, multiply, rows, times**

Multiplication is a short way to calculate repeated additions.

$$5 + 5 + 5 + 5 = 4 \textbf{ lots of } 5 = 20$$

Times one number by another to get the answer and make the calculation more efficient. The symbol for multiplication is $\times$.

Example:

Question: What is 5 multiplied by 6?

Answer: $5 \times 6 = 30$

We use an **array** of **rows** and **columns** to show how this works.

$$5 + 5 + 5 = 3 \times 5 = 15 \quad \text{or} \quad 3 + 3 + 3 + 3 + 3 = 5 \times 3 = 15$$

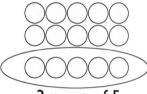

3 rows of 5

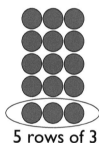

5 rows of 3

Language focus!
Multiplication words

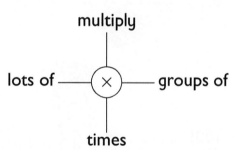

multiply

lots of —— $\times$ —— groups of

times

As the array shows, changing the order of the numbers in the multiplication does not change the answer.

Think about it!

1. **What is 3 times 4?** _____

2. **Multiply 9 by 5.** _____

Practise it!

1. Which multiplication questions do these arrays represent?

(a)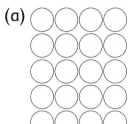

(b)

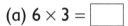   _____

2. Write a number in each box to make these number sentences correct.

(a) $6 \times 3 = \boxed{}$

(b) $\boxed{} \times 5 = 40$

(c) 10 lots of $\boxed{} = 90$

(d) 3 times $\boxed{} = 21$

3. Solve these word problems.

(a) There are 5 fingers on one hand.

How many fingers are there on 3 hands?

_____

(b) A classroom has 6 tables.

4 students sit at each table.

How many students are in the class?

_____

(c) There are 15 pencils in a pack.

How many pencils are there in 4 packs?

_____

(d) A teacher puts students into groups of 10.

There are 4 groups.

How many students are there altogether?

_____

Teachers' and parents' note

Encourage students to draw arrays to help with their initial calculations and to ensure that they understand that multiplication is commutative (gives the same answer with the numbers in any order). Ask pupils to write their own multiplication questions using all the different vocabulary.

Division

Read it!

Key words: divide, even, groups of, left over, odd, remainder, share equally

Division is splitting a number into equal parts.

The number is **shared equally** into groups.

The symbol for **division** is ÷

Example: Here is a bowl of 20 cherries.
Question: 5 people share the cherries equally.
How many cherries does 1 person get?
Answer: 4 cherries

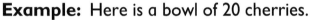

Even numbers
divide exactly by 2.
$12 ÷ 2 = 6$

Odd numbers
do not **divide** exactly by 2.
$9 ÷ 2 = 4 r 1$
This is also written as $4\frac{1}{2}$

1 **left over**

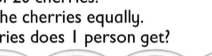

split this into
2 equal parts

giving $\frac{1}{2}$

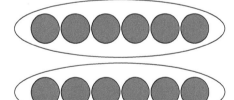

2 groups of 6

2 groups of 4

Language focus!

Finding a fraction is the same as dividing into equal parts.
halve = divide into 2 equal parts
third = divide into 3 equal parts
quarter = divide into 4 equal parts

Sometimes a number will not divide exactly as shown in the diagram below. There is one left over. This is called a remainder.
$10 ÷ 3 = 3 r 1$

remainder

Think about it!

1. **Divide 15 by 5.**

_____

2. **Share 24 into 4 equal groups.**

_____

3. **What is the remainder when 17 is divided by 3?**

_____

Practise it!

1. **Draw a ring around the numbers that divide exactly by 10.**

   50   35   20   40   79   60

2. **Divide each of these numbers by 2.**

   (a) 18 _____   (b) 7 _____

   (c) 26 _____   (d) 15 _____

3. **Solve these word problems.**

   (a) Sally and Lulu share 30 beads equally.

   How many beads does Sally have? _____

   (b) 33 children are put into groups of 3.

   How many groups will there be? _____

   (c) Bruno has 72 stickers.

   He puts 10 stickers on each page in a book.

   How many stickers are left over? _____

   (d) A farmer has 38 apples.

   He puts 5 apples into each bag.

   How many apples are left over? _____

Teachers' and parents' note

Give students practical experience of dividing counters, beads or other small objects into groups of 2, 3, 5 and 10. Divide the class into groups of 3, 4 and 5 and see how many students are left over.

Doubles and halves

Read it!

Key words: double, half, halve, inverse, opposite

Double means 'multiply a number by 2'.

Halve means 'divide a number by 2'.

Example:
Question: What is 3 doubled?
Answer: 6

Example:
Question: What is half of 8?
Answer: 4

Doubling and halving can both help us to solve mental calculations more easily.

Example:
Question: How is the 2 times table used to make the 4 times table?

Answer:

2 times table	2	4	6	8	10	12
				double ↓		
4 times table	4	8	12	16	20	24

Halving is the **opposite** or **inverse** of **doubling**.

Double the 5 times table to get the 10 times table.

5	10	15	20	25	30
10	20	30	40	50	60

Halve the 10 times table to get the 5 times table.

10	20	30	40	50	60
5	10	15	20	25	30

Language focus!

opposite operations

double 4 is 8 ⇐ inverse ⇒ half of 8 is 4

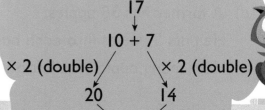

Partition larger numbers to help you double.

```
        17
        ↓
      10 + 7
 × 2 (double)   × 2 (double)
      20        14
         34
```

Think about it!

What is double 18? _____   **What is half of 30?** _____

Practise it!

1. Leroy has 3 boxes of apples.

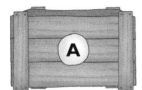

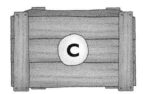

12 apples   26 apples   18 apples

He takes half of the apples out of each box.

How many apples does he take out of each box?

Box A: _____ apples   Box B: _____ apples   Box C: _____ apples

2. Fill in the circle.
Double each number.

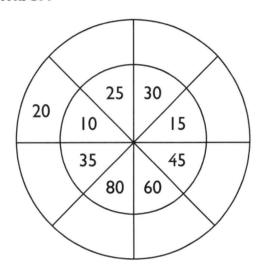

3. Complete the table.

Number	50	250	400	150	300
Double the number					

Number	16	10	11	12	38
Halve the number					

Teachers' and parents' note

Encourage students to use doubling and halving to develop the link between the 2 and 4 times tables and the 5 and 10 times tables. Make sure that they know that halving is the inverse of doubling.

Times tables

Key words: division, inverse, multiple, multiplication, times table

A **times table** is a collection of all the **multiplication** facts for one number. The answers are called the **multiples** of that number.

2 times table

$1 \times 2 = 2$
$2 \times 2 = 4$
$3 \times 2 = 6$
$4 \times 2 = 8$
$5 \times 2 = 10$
$6 \times 2 = 12$
$7 \times 2 = 14$
$8 \times 2 = 16$
$9 \times 2 = 18$
$10 \times 2 = 20$

multiples of 2

So 2, 4, 6, 8, 10, 12 … are the **multiples** of 2.

Example:
Question: Write the first 4 multiples of 5.
Answer: 5, 10, 15, 20

Division is the **inverse** or opposite of **multiplication**.
So the **times tables** also give us **division** facts.

$6 \times 2 = 12$ so $12 \div 2 = 6$
or $12 \div 6 = 2$

Language focus!

Everyday meaning of **table**: a piece of furniture with a flat top and 3 or more legs

Mathematical meaning of **table**: a set of figures shown in rows and columns

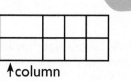

row→

↑column

The link between multiplication and division means each table fact gives us 3 others.
$3 \times 5 = 15$ so $5 \times 3 = 15$
and $15 \div 3 = 5$
and $15 \div 5 = 3$

6

Think about it!

Write the division problems that could be solved with these multiplication facts.

$3 \times 4 = 12$ $7 \times 5 = 35$ $8 \times 10 = 80$

_____   _____   _____

_____   _____   _____

Practise it!

1. Draw a ring around the multiples of 3 in this list.

      6   15   11   9   25   21

2. Aisha has some number and operation cards.

    | 3 | | 10 | | 30 | | × | | ÷ | | = |

She uses them to make a number sentence.

    | 3 | × | 10 | = | 30 |

She changes the cards to make a different number sentence.
What could the sentence be?
Give 3 answers. _____

_____

_____

3. Use multiplication and division facts to solve these word problems.

(a) There are 5 buttons on a coat.
How many buttons are there on 5 coats?

_____

(b) Notebooks are sold in packs of 10.
A teacher needs 30 notebooks for her class.
How many packs does she need?

_____

(c) There are 3 people in a team for a times table challenge.
There are 7 teams in the challenge.
How many people are there in the challenge?

Times table challenge

_____

Teachers' and parents' note

Ask students to learn the 2, 3, 5 and 10 times tables and say them out loud.
Ensure that students link these to giving division facts.
Ask students to list multiples of these numbers out loud.

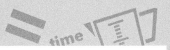

Word problems

Read it!

Key words: answer, number sentence, operation, word problem

A **word problem** is a mathematical problem from real life.
It begins in words but can be rewritten using a **number sentence**.
It uses an **operation** such as **addition**, **subtraction**, **multiplication**, **division** or **fractions**.

Example:
Question: A toy maker puts 4 wheels on a toy car. How many cars does he make with 20 wheels?
Answer: 20 ÷ 4 = 5 cars

Some word problems use more than one calculation to find the **answer**. These are called two step problems.

Example: A car park has 30 spaces.
There are 15 cars and 4 vans parked in the car park.
How many spaces are there?

Answer:
calculation 1	or	calculation 2
15 + 4 = 19		30 − 15 = 15
30 − 19 = 11		15 − 4 = 11

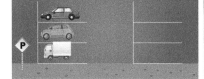

Language focus!
Operation words

+	−	×	÷
addition	subtraction	multiplication	division
add	subtract	multiply	divide
altogether	decrease	groups of	shared
and	difference	lots of	(equally)
increase	minus	times	
more than	less than		
plus	take away		

• Read the problem carefully.
• Decide the steps needed to solve the problem.
• Work out the answer.
• Check that the answer makes sense.

Think about it!

Match the word problem to the calculation needed to solve it.

| Lulu had 10 pencils. She lost 5 of them. How many pencils does she have now? | What is the difference between 10 and 5? | 10 boys and 5 girls line up at the door. How many students are in the line? |

$10 + 5$ $10 - 5$

Practise it!

1. Which operation would you use to solve these problems?
Write $+$, $-$, $\times$ or $\div$.

(a) There are 42 sheep in a field.

The farmer takes 15 away.

How many sheep are left? _____

(b) 3 friends share 21 stickers equally.

How many do they get each? _____

2. Solve these word problems.

(a) There are 12 apples in a bowl.

$\frac{1}{4}$ of them are red. The rest are green.

How many apples are green? _____

(b) A buttercup has 5 petals.

How many petals do 6 buttercups have? _____

Teachers' and parents' note

Give students experience of word problems using all the possible vocabulary. Ask them to identify the operations needed to solve the problems using operation cards or mini-whiteboards.

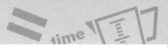

2D shapes

Read it!

Key words: circle, rectangle, semicircle, square, triangle, classify, property, edge, side, vertex, vertices

A 2D shape is made of **sides** and **vertices**.

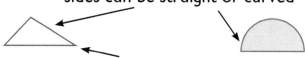

sides can be straight or curved

a vertex is where sides meet

Shapes are **classified** using **properties** such as the number of **vertices** or the type of **side**, for example all shapes with 3 straight **sides** and 3 **vertices** are **triangles**.

Example:
Question: Which shape has 1 curved side?
Answer: A circle.

Language focus!

Singular	Plural
edge	edges
side	sides
vertex	vertices
property	properties

Not all 4-sided shapes are squares or rectangles.

A square has 4 equal sides and 4 right angles.

A rectangle has 4 sides and 4 right angles. The opposite sides are equal.

This shape has 4 sides. It is not a square or a rectangle.

Think about it!

Put a tick (✓) in the shapes that are squares.

Practise it!

1. Count the vertices on each shape.

Write your answer below each shape.

 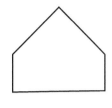 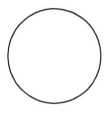 

_____ vertices   _____ vertices   _____ vertices   _____ vertices

2. Here is a picture of a cat.

Colour all the triangles yellow.

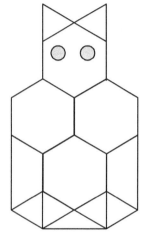

3. Here is a list of some of the properties of a shape.

It has straight sides.

It has 4 vertices.

It has curved sides.

It has a right angle.

It has 2 vertices.

Write the properties of a semicircle. _____

_____

Regular shapes

Read it!

Key words: classify, irregular, hexagon, octagon, pentagon, regular

All the sides on a **regular** shape are the same length.

regular triangle   regular hexagon

All other shapes are **irregular**.

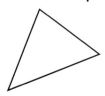 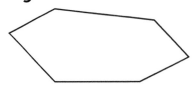

irregular triangle   irregular hexagon

Example:
Question: Is this shape regular or irregular?
Answer: Regular

Language focus!
Names of shapes

Number of sides	Name of shape
5	pentagon
6	hexagon
8	octagon

A regular 4-sided shape is called a square.

Think about it!

Put a tick (✓) in the regular shapes.

Practise it!

1. Draw a line to show which group each shape belongs to.

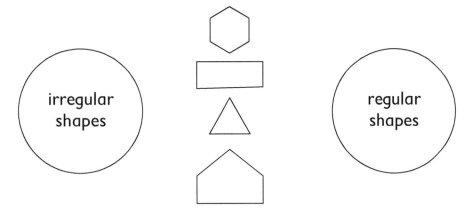

irregular shapes

regular shapes

2. Name these shapes.

Remember to say if they are regular or irregular.

(a)   (b)   (c)   (d)

_____   _____   _____   _____

_____   _____   _____   _____

3. Use the triangular grid to draw a regular hexagon and an irregular octagon.

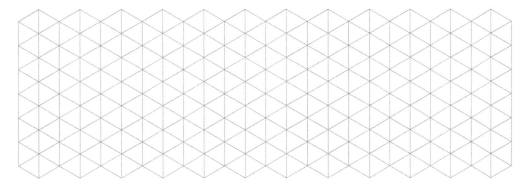

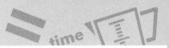

Right angles

Read it!

Key words: angle, right angle, turn, straight line

An **angle** measures how far something **turns**.
A **right angle** is a quarter of a whole **turn**.

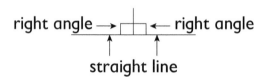

whole turn   right angles   straight line

A **straight line** is made from two right angles.

The symbol ⌐ is used to show a **right angle**.

Example:
Question: How many of the angles in this shape are right angles?
Answer: 2

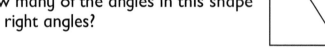

The vertices in **squares** and rectangles are always **right angles**.

Other shapes may have vertices that are **right angles**.

Language focus!
Right angle

An angle that makes a quarter of a turn to the **left** is still called a right angle. A left angle does **not** exist.

To make a useful right angle, fold any piece of paper into four like this.

You can use your right angle to check the size of other angles.

Think about it!

Put a tick (✓) in the shapes that have at least one right angle. Put the tick in one of the right angles.

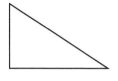    

Practise it!

1. Here are four angles.

A.   B.   C.    D.

Which angles are right angles? Write A, B, C or D. _____

2. Circle 3 right angles you can see in this kitchen.

One has been done for you.

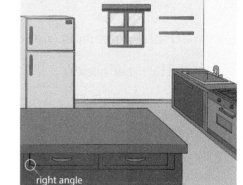
right angle

3. Use the square grid to draw:

(a) a pentagon that has two right-angled vertices

(b) a hexagon with one right-angled vertex

Mark the right angles clearly with this symbol: ☐

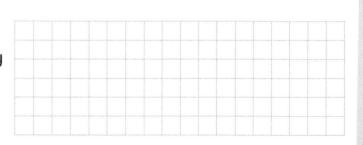

Teachers' and parents' note

Encourage students to use a familiar right angle such as the corner of a book to check if an angle really is a right angle. Give them experience of drawing right angles together to make a straight line.

Line symmetry

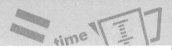

Read it!

Key words: line of symmetry, mirror line, reflection, symmetrical, symmetry

A **line of symmetry** splits a shape or image into two identical pieces. One half is a **reflection** of the other.

The **line of symmetry** is also called the **mirror line** because of this property.

Example:

Question: Draw the line of symmetry on this shape.

Answer:

A **symmetrical** pattern is made by reflecting a design in a mirror line.

design reflection

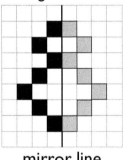

mirror line

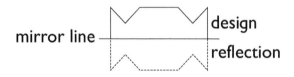

mirror line

design

reflection

Language focus!

Symmetrical shapes

Shapes that have at least one line of symmetry are called symmetrical shapes. Lines of symmetry are also called mirror lines.

If you fold a shape along a line of symmetry, the two parts will overlap exactly.

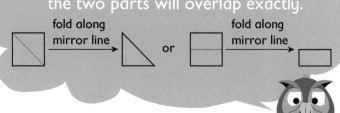

fold along mirror line   or   fold along mirror line

Think about it!

Put a tick (✓) in the symmetrical shapes.

Practise it!

1. Draw a line of symmetry on each of these shapes.

  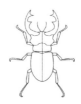

2. Draw the reflection of these images in the mirror line.

What shape does it make? Write the name under the image.

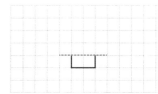   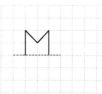

_____ _____ _____ _____

3. Reflect the pattern in the mirror line to complete the symmetrical design.

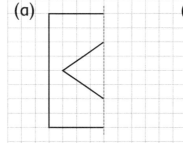 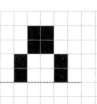

Teachers' and parents' note

Look for symmetrical objects and patterns in the environment. Give students practical experience of using a mirror to find and create symmetrical patterns. Ask pupils to fold paper shapes such as squares, triangles and rectangles to find their lines of symmetry.

45

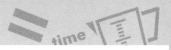

3D shapes

Read it!

Key words: cone, cube, cuboid, cylinder, sphere, curved, edge, face, flat, vertices

A 3D shape is made from **faces**, **edges** and **vertices**.

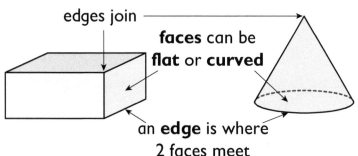

a **vertex** is where
edges join

faces can be
flat or **curved**

an **edge** is where
2 faces meet

Example: Here is a cube.

Question: How many faces does it have?
Answer: 6 faces

Shapes with flat faces	Shapes with some curved faces

  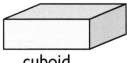

cube   cuboid

cone   cylinder   sphere

Language focus!

Singular	Plural
face	faces
edge	edges
vertex	vertices

The flat faces on 3D shapes are usually common 2D shapes. A cuboid is made from 6 rectangles. A cylinder has 2 flat faces, which are circles, and a curved face.

Think about it!

Write the name of the 3D shape under each object.

(a)

(b)

(c)
beans

(d)

_____ _____ _____ _____

Practise it!

I. Draw a line to join each shape to its name.

cube   cylinder   sphere   cone   cuboid

2. Here is a picture of a robot made from 3D shapes.

(a) Colour the cuboids blue.

(b) Colour the cones red.

(c) Colour the cylinders yellow.

(d) Colour the cubes green.

(e) Colour the sphere purple.

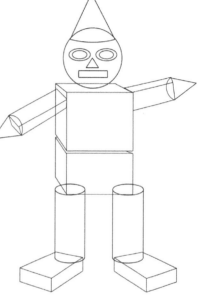

3. Complete the table.
One row has been done for you.

	Number of flat faces	Number of curved faces	Number of vertices
cube	6	0	8
cylinder			
cuboid			
cone			

Teachers' and parents' note

Look for 3D shapes in the environment. Discuss the types of faces and count the number of edges and vertices. Put a 3D shape in a bag so that it cannot be seen. Ask a student to feel the shape and describe it without mentioning its name. Can another student work out the name of the shape?

Pyramids and prisms

Read it!

Key words: base, edge, face, prism, pyramid, vertex

A **pyramid** is a 3D shape with a straight-sided 2D **base** and triangular **faces** that join at a **vertex**.

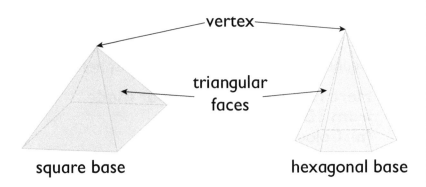

vertex

triangular faces

square base

hexagonal base

A **prism** is a 3D shape that has end **faces** that are the same shape and rectangular **faces** in the middle.

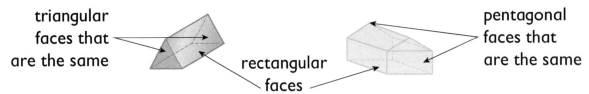

triangular faces that are the same

rectangular faces

pentagonal faces that are the same

The 2D shape on the **base** of the **pyramid** or the end **face** of a **prism** gives the shape its name.

Example:

Question: Is this shape a pyramid or a prism?

Answer: A prism.

Language focus!

Base or end face	Pyramid	Prism
△	triangular pyramid	triangular prism
□	square based pyramid	cuboid
⬡	hexagonal pyramid	hexagonal prism

If you cut a prism along its length, the shape will be the same as the end faces.

Think about it!

1. **Draw a ring around the shapes that are pyramids.**

2. **Write the name of each shape below it.**

(a)    (b)   (c)   (d)

_____   _____   _____   _____

Practise it!

1. **Habib says:** "There is a shape in this bag.
One of its faces is a pentagon.
Five of its faces are triangles."

What is the name of Habib's shape?

_____

2. **Here are some labels.**

Use the labels to complete the table. Write each label only once.

| faces |
| triangular prism |
| vertices |
| square based pyramid |

	edges		
	9	5	6
	8	5	5
octagonal prism	24	10	16

Nets

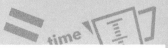

Read it!

Key words: edge, face, net

A **net** is a flat shape that will fold to give a 3D shape.

This **net** has square **faces**.

It will fold to make a cube.

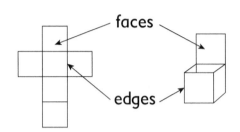

faces

edges

Example:

Question: How many square faces make the net of a cube?

Answer: 6

Not all groups of 6 squares make a cube.

nets that will make a cube   nets that will **not** make a cube

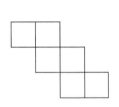

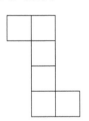

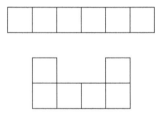

Language focus!

Everyday meaning of **net**: a mesh used to catch fish or a lacy curtain

Mathematical meaning of **net**: a 2D shape that folds to give a 3D shape

Some nets with 5 squares will make a cube without a lid. This is called an **open** cube.

Think about it!

Tick (✓) the nets that will make a cube.

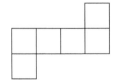

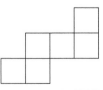

Practise it!

1. Sven is drawing the net of a cube.

 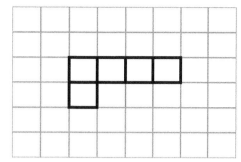

Draw the sixth square to complete the net.

2. Draw a line to join each diagram to the correct group.

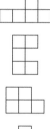

will make an open cube		will not make an open cube

3. Use the square grid to draw a net that will make a closed cube.

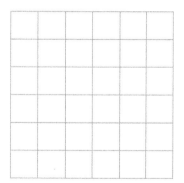

Teachers' and parents' note

Unfold packets that are cubes to demonstrate how a 3D shape becomes a net. Allow students to experiment with squares that join together to find nets that make open and closed cubes.

Position and movement

Read it!

Key words: above, below, down, left, position, right, route, up

The **position** of an object shows where it is in relation to other objects.

←——— left   right ———→

In the diagram the circle is to the **left** of the rectangle and the triangle is to the **right** of the square.

Here the beans are **above** the flour and the juice is **below** the rice.

Example:

Question: Look at the picture.
Is the juice to the left or to the right of the flour?

Answer: To the left.

Movement changes the position of an object in different ways.

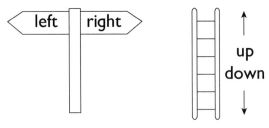

up
down

Language focus!

Opposites

left	right
up	down
above	below

Up and down are also used to show movement on a paper diagram.

Think about it!

Look at the animals in the picture.

1. Which animal is on the left of the rabbit?

_____

2. Which animal is on the right of the rabbit?

_____

Practise it!

1. Here are some shapes.

(a) Write the letter X above the circle.

(b) Write the letter Y below the hexagon.

(c) Write the letter Z to the left of the octagon.

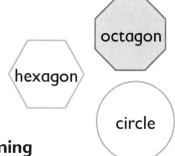

octagon

hexagon

circle

2. Mia plans a route from her house to the swimming pool on the map.

Mia's route:
Go up School Lane.
Turn left into Main Road.
Turn right into the pool.

Lucy takes the shortest route to school. Write the route that Lucy takes to get to school.

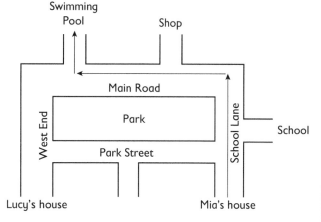

_____

_____

_____

Teachers' and parents' note

Use objects in the classroom to give practical experience of above, below, left and right.

Ask students to move left and right and turn clockwise and anticlockwise by quarter, half and three quarter turns.

Using grids

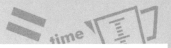

Read it!

Key words: column, down, grid, left, position, right, row, up

A **grid** is made of **rows**

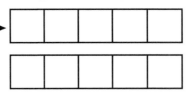

and **columns** of squares. These are labelled using numbers or letters.

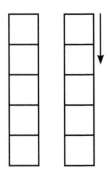

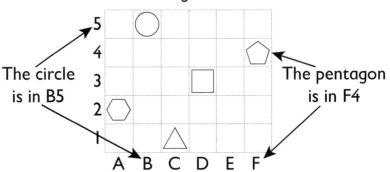

The circle is in B5

The pentagon is in F4

The **position** of an object is written using the labels for the square it is in.

Example: Look at the diagram above.
Question: Which shape is in D3?
Answer: The square.

Language focus!

Everyday meanings of **column**:
a round pillar

or a section in a newspaper

Mathematical meaning of **column**:
the squares in a grid going up.

To find the position, first go along (the corridor) and then up (the stairs).

Think about it!

Here is a grid made of squares.

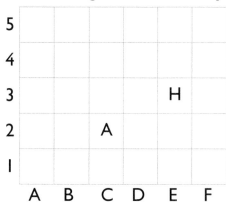

1. Write the letter S in square F1.

2. Write the letter T in square D4.

3. Write the letter M in square B3.

4. Which letter is in column C? _____

5. Which letter is in row 3? _____

Practise it!

1. **Here is a grid made of squares.**

   Write the position of:

   (a) the apple

   (b) the banana

   (c) the orange

   (d) the strawberry

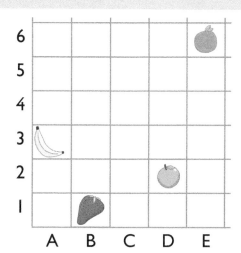

2. **In the grid the tree is in square A4 and the boat is in square D2.**

   Label the rows and columns using letters A–E and numbers 1–4.

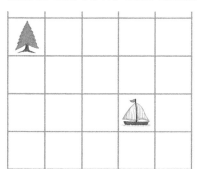

Teachers' and parents' note

Ensure that students give the across position followed by the up position in their answers as this will make the transition to using coordinates easier.

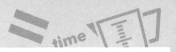

Length

Read it!

Key words: height, length, long, ruler, tall, wide, width, centimetres, kilometres, metres

Length is the measurement of the distance between two points.

Length is measured in **centimetres**, **metres** and **kilometres**.

length

width

height

Small objects are measured in **centimetres** with a **ruler**.	Larger objects or short distances are measured in **metres**.	The distance between two towns is measured in **kilometres**.

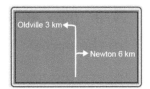

Oldville 3 km
Newton 6 km

Language focus!

Finding a ...	Question
length	How long?
width	How wide?
height	How tall?

When you are asked to measure a width or height your answer will be a measure of **length**.

Think about it!

1. **Which units would you use to measure these items?**
   Write centimetres, metres or kilometres under each picture.

(a)

(b)

(c)

(d)

· Oxford

London

_____   _____   _____   _____

Practise it!

1. Look carefully at the diagram.

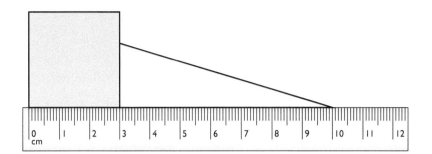

1. How long are the two shapes altogether?

   _____

2. What is the length of the triangle?

   _____

3. How much longer is the triangle than the square?

   _____

2. Use a ruler to measure the height of these flowers.
Write the height under each flower.

(a)

_____

(b)

_____

(c)

_____

(d)

_____

3. May has 150 cm of red ribbon.
She uses 85 cm. How much does she have left?

_____

Mass

Key words: balance, gram, heavy, kilogram, light, scales, weigh

Mass is the measurement of the weight of items such as flour or rice. It is measured in **kilograms** or **grams**.

Example:
Question: What is the mass of the apples?
Answer: 1 kilogram or 1 kg

Light items or small amounts are measured in **grams**.

Heavy items or large amounts are measured in **kilograms**.

Language focus!
Focus words
Comparative/Superlative adjectives

| light $\rightarrow$ lighter $\rightarrow$ the lightest |
| heavy $\rightarrow$ heavier $\rightarrow$ the heaviest |

1 kilogram is equal to 1000 grams.
We write this as
1 kg = 1000 g.

Tim weighs two pumpkins.   A   B

1. What is the mass of pumpkin A? _____

2. How much lighter is pumpkin B? _____

3. What is the total mass of the two pumpkins? _____

Practise it!

1. Draw a ring around the heavier item on each balance.

(a) 　　(b) 　　(c)

2. Which units would you use to measure these?
Write kilograms or grams under each picture.

(a) 　　(b) 　　(c)

_____　　　　_____　　　　_____

3. Kojo makes a cake.

(a) He weighs out the flour.
What is the mass of the flour? _____

(b) He adds 200 g of sugar to the scales.
Draw an arrow to show the mass on the scales now.

Teachers' and parents' note

Give students practical experience of mass using scales and balances. Ask them to estimate the mass of items such as apples and then weigh them to check the real mass. Discuss the mass of familiar packets, bags and cartons of food such as rice or flour.

Capacity

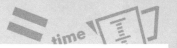

Read it!

Key words: empty, full, litre, millilitre, contains, pours

Capacity is the measurement of liquids like water or orange juice.
It is measured using **litres** (l) and **millilitres** (ml).

Example: Here is a jug.

Question: What is the capacity of the jug
when it is full?
Answer: 2 litres.

Language focus!
Opposites

full

empty

I litre is equal to 1000 millilitres.
We write this as 1l = 1000 ml

Think about it!

Here is a bucket of water.

1. How much water is in the bucket? _____

2. What is the capacity of the
bucket when it is full? _____

3. Jack pours more water into
the bucket. How much more
water will fill the bucket? _____

Practise it!

1. Which units would you use to measure these liquids?
Write litres or millilitres.

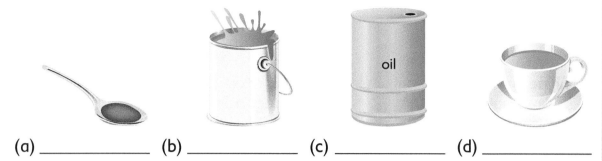

(a) _____ (b) _____ (c) _____ (d) _____

2. This beaker holds $\frac{1}{2}$ l.

This bowl holds 3 l.

Kara uses the beaker to fill the bowl.

How many full beakers will she need? _____

3. Rohan has 2 cartons of juice.

He pours them both into this jug.

(a) Draw a line on the jug to show
the level of the juice.

(b) Rohan pours 1 l of the juice into
some glasses.
How much juice is left? _____

Teachers' and parents' note

Encourage students to experiment with different containers to develop a better understanding of this measurement. Get them to fill the containers with water and empty them. They should also try filling larger containers with smaller ones.

Ask: How many cups fill the bottle?
How many teaspoons fill the glass?

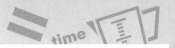

Telling the time

Read it!

Key words: **analogue clock, digital clock, past, to, day, hour, minute, second**

Time is the measurement of how long it takes to do something.
It is measured in **hours, minutes** and **seconds**.
It is measured on:

an analogue clock   **a digital clock**

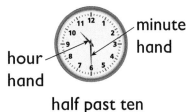

minute hand

hour hand

half past ten

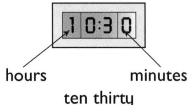

hours   minutes

ten thirty

Example:
Question: What time does this clock show?
Answer: Half past two or two thirty.

On **analogue clocks** the words **past** (the last hour) and **to** (the next hour) are used to read the time.

On **digital clocks** the time is read using numbers.

eleven twenty or
twenty **past** eleven

three fifty or
ten **to** four

Language focus!

1 day = 24 hours
1 hour = 60 minutes
1 minute = 60 seconds

15 minutes is a quarter of an hour so one fifteen can be read as quarter past one, and five forty-five can be read as quarter to six.

Think about it!

Write the time for each analogue clock using the words *past* and *to*.

(a)

(b)

(c)

(d)

_____   _____   _____   _____

Practise it!

1. **Draw lines to match each time to the correct digital clock.**

   half past eight   `05:10`

   twenty five to eleven   `10:35`

   quarter to three   `08:30`

   ten past five   `02:45`

2. **Here is a clock at the station.**
   The next train leaves in 20 minutes.
   What time does the train leave?

   _____

3. **A film lasts for $1\frac{1}{2}$ hours.**
   It starts at 6:35.
   What time does it finish?

   _____

Teachers' and parents' note

Give students the opportunity to read analogue and digital times aloud to ensure that they understand how the words 'past' and 'to' are used. Make sure they can see that the hour hand continues to move slowly during an hour on an analogue clock. It only points exactly to a digit on the hour. At half past two it should be exactly half way between the digits 2 and 3.

Using a calendar

Read it!

Key words: calendar, date, day, month, week, year

Longer periods of time are measured in **days**, **weeks**, **months** and **years**.
A **calendar** is a set of tables that show:

the **date**
what day and
month it is

or

a **month**
split into
days and weeks

day — Monday
6
month — July

days of
the week

There are 7 **days** in a **week**:
Monday, Tuesday, Wednesday,
Thursday, Friday, Saturday and Sunday.

Example: Look at the calendar
for January.
Question: What date is the last Monday in January?
Answer: 27th of January

Some **calendars** show all 12 **months** for one **year** on one page.
The **months** have different numbers of **days**.

January	February	March	April
31	28(29)	31	30
May	June	July	August
31	30	31	31
September	October	November	December
30	31	30	31

Here is a
rhyme to
help you
remember
this.

30 days has September,
April, June and November.
All the rest have 31
Except February alone
Which has 28 days clear
And 29 in a leap year.

Language focus!

one week = 7 days
one year = 12 months
one year = 52 weeks
one year = 365 days
leap year = 366 days

Most years have 365
days but leap years
have 366 days. A leap
year happens every 4
years. In a leap year
February has 29 days.

Think about it!

Look at the calendar for January at the top of this page.

1. What day of the week is 7th January?

_____

2. What date is the third Thursday in January?

_____

Practise it!

1. Here is a blank page from a calendar.

1st June is on a Monday.

Complete the calendar for June.

	JUNE					
SUN	**MON**	**TUE**	**WED**	**THU**	**FRI**	**SAT**

(a) What day is 13th June?

_____

(b) What date is the last Friday in June?

_____

(c) What day is 1st July?

_____

2. The calendar shows today's date.

(a) What day is 15th April?

_____

(b) What is the date next Sunday?

_____

SUNDAY
11th
April

3. Here are two pages from a calendar.

(a) What day is 23rd October?

_____

(b) What is the date on the second Monday in September?

_____

SEPTEMBER						
SUN	MON	TUE	WED	THU	FRI	SAT
				1	2	3
4	5	6	7	8	9	10
11	12	13	14	15	16	17
18	19	20	21	22	23	24
25	26	27	28	29	30	

(c) What day is 1st November?

_____

(d) How long is it from 25th September to 5th October?

_____

OCTOBER						
SUN	MON	TUE	WED	THU	FRI	SAT
		1	2	3	4	5
6	7	8	9	10	11	12
13	14	15	16	17	18	19
20	21	22	23	24	25	26
27	28	29	30			

(e) What is the date 3 weeks after/from 3rd September?

_____

Teachers' and parents' note

Show students different types of calendars and discuss how they are set out.

Ask them to learn the rhyme and say it out loud to help them remember the number of days in each month.

Using measurements

Read it!

Key words: compare, estimate, measurement, measuring jug, ruler, scales, centimetre, metre, kilometre, grams, kilograms, millilitres, litres

A **measurement** is the size of an object.
It is measured using equipment such as a **ruler**, **scales** or a **measuring jug**.

| ruler | kitchen scales | measuring jug |

Sometimes an exact **measurement** is not needed and an **estimate** is used.
An **estimate** is a guess based on known information.

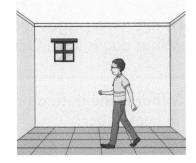

Example: A man's stride is about 1 metre.
So the room is about 6 m long.
Question: How wide is the room?
Answer: about 4 m

Language focus!

Measurement	Comparison words
length	longest or shortest
width	widest or narrowest
height	tallest or shortest
mass	heaviest or lightest
capacity	largest or smallest

Remember the units that are used for each measurement.

Measurement	Units of measurement
length/width/ height	100 centimetres = 1 metre 1000 metres = 1 kilometre
mass	1000 grams = 1 kilogram
capacity	1000 millilitres = 1 litre

Think about it!

1. **Estimate the size of each object.**
   Draw a ring around the correct object in each case.

   (a) Which is heavier?   (b) Which is shorter?   (c) Which is taller?

   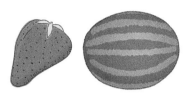      

Practise it!

1. **Solve these word problems. Write a number sentence to show your answer.**

   (a) A sunflower plant measures 195 cm tall.

   It grows 9 cm more in a week.

   How tall is it now?

   _____

   (b) A painter has a 5-litre tin of paint.

   He uses $\frac{1}{2}$ of the paint in the tin to

   paint the kitchen.
   How much paint is left?

   _____

   (c) Jamil has 1 kilogram of rice.

   He uses 400 grams.

   How much rice does he have left?

   _____

Teachers' and parents' note

Give students practical experience of estimating measurements by comparing objects with other objects that have a known measurement, such as a ruler or a 500 g weight. Then ask them to measure the objects accurately to improve their estimating skills.

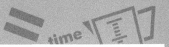

Tally charts

Read it!

Key words: frequency table, represent, tally, tally chart, total

A **tally chart** is used to count real life information, such as the number of different creatures in a pond or the colour of cars in a car park.

Colour of car	Tally	Total
red	卌 ||	7
blue	||||	4
black	卌	5

Example: Look at the tally chart.
Question: How many black cars are there in the car park?
Answer: 5

Each mark **represents** I car

Tally marks are just lines used to count each object.
To make counting simple, the fifth line is drawn across the previous four.

|	||	|||	||||	卌	卌|	卌||	卌|||	卌||||	卌卌
1	2	3	4	5	6	7	8	9	10

Language focus!

Singular	Plural
tally	tallies
frequency	frequencies
total	totals

A table of information without the tally marks is called a **frequency table**.

Colour of car	Frequency
red	7
blue	4
black	5

Think about it!

This tally chart shows students' favourite fruit.

1. How many people like apples? _____

2. How many people like oranges? _____

3. How many more people like strawberries than bananas? _____

Fruit	Tally
apple	卌 卌 ||
banana	卌 ||||
orange	卌 |
strawberry	卌 卌 卌

Practise it!

1. Here is a set of shapes.

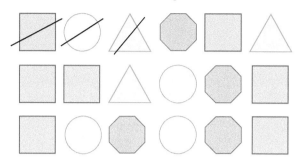

shape	tally	total
circle	I	
hexagon		
square	I	
triangle	I	

Complete the tally chart for this information. The first three tallies have been done for you.

2. Here are two frequency tables to show students' favourite sports.

Boys	
Sport	**Frequency**
football	15
gymnastics	6
hockey	3
swimming	10
tennis	8

Girls	
Sport	**Frequency**
football	7
gymnastics	10
hockey	5
swimming	12
tennis	8

(a) How many boys like hockey? _____

(b) How many girls like swimming? _____

(c) How many more girls than boys like gymnastics? _____

(d) How many students altogether like football? _____

Teachers' and parents' note

Give students practical experience of collecting information in a tally chart, such as tallying the number of students born in each month, or combine with a science project to count the number of small animals in different locations.

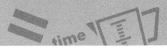

Bar charts

Read it!

Key words: axis, bar chart, horizontal, label, scale, title, vertical

A **bar chart** uses rectangular **bars** to show real life information, such as the colour of students' eyes or their favourite fruit.

It is drawn using **horizontal** and **vertical axes**.

Each **axis** has a **label** to show what the **bars** represent.

Each **bar chart** must have a **title** to show what information is displayed.

Example: Look at the bar chart.
Question: How many people have brown eyes?
Answer: 9 people.

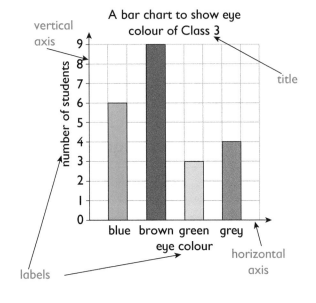

The **scale** in the **bar chart** above counts up in ones.

The **scale** on this **bar chart** counts up in twos as it displays larger numbers.

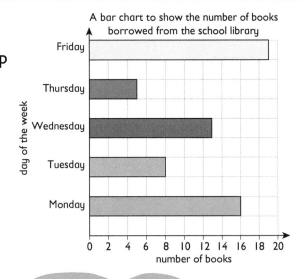

Language focus!

Singular	Plural
axis	axes
bar	bars
label	labels

The **bars** in a **bar chart** can be **vertical** or **horizontal**, as shown in the two bar charts above.

Think about it!

Look at the bar chart about the school library.

1. How many books were borrowed on Tuesday?

_____

2. How many more books were borrowed on Monday than Thursday?

_____

Practise it!

1. **Here is a bar chart to show the favourite colours of Class 3.**

   (a) How many students like blue?

   _____

   (b) Which colour did 2 students choose?

   _____

   (c) How many students are there in Class 3?

   _____

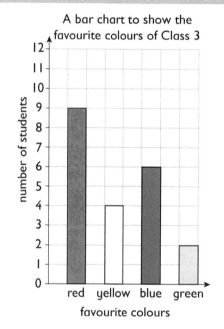

A bar chart to show the favourite colours of Class 3

2. **Four friends went swimming.**
   Look at how many lengths they swam.

Name	Number of lengths
Max	4
Joe	6
Sid	7
Tom	5

   Draw bars to show this information in the chart below.

   The first one has been done for you.

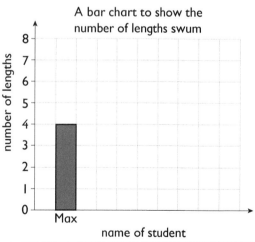

A bar chart to show the number of lengths swum

Teachers' and parents' note

Look for vertical and horizontal lines in the environment to develop an understanding of these words.
Give students the opportunity to collect their own data and display it in a bar chart.

Pictograms

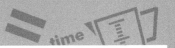

Read it!

Key words: key, list, pictogram, represents (stands for), symbol, title

A **pictogram** uses pictures as **symbols** to **represent** information.

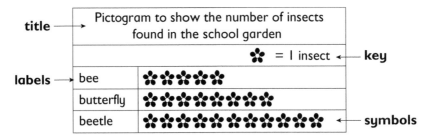

Each **pictogram** has a **key** to tell you what the **symbol** represents (stands for) and a **title** to tell you what the information is about.

Example: Look at the pictogram above.

Question: How many butterflies did they find?

Answer: 8 butterflies.

In the **pictogram** above, the **symbol** stands for 1 insect but it can represent other data.

In this **pictogram** the **symbol** stands for 2 pieces of fruit.

Picture to show the amount of fruit sold at the school shop	
	👥 = 2 pieces of fruit
apple	👥👥👥👥👥👥👥👥👥👥👥👥👥
banana	👥👥👥👥👥👥👥👥👥
orange	👥👥👥👥👥👥
pear	👥👥👥

Language focus!

Everyday meaning of **key**: a device used to open a lock.

Mathematical meaning of **key**: a guide to colours or symbols used in a graph

Always look carefully at the key to make sure you understand what the symbol represents.

Think about it!

Look at the pictogram about the fruit sold in the school shop.

1. How many bananas did they sell? _____

2. How many oranges did they sell? _____

3. How many more apples than pears did they sell? _____

Practise it!

1. Here is a pictogram.

Pictogram to show the number of days of sunshine in each month	
	☀ = 2 days
February	☀☀☀☀☀☀☀
March	☀☀☀☀☀☀☀☀
April	☀☀☀☀☀☀
May	☀☀☀☀☀☀☀☀☀☀

(a) Which month had 14 sunny days? _____

(b) How many of the days in March were sunny? _____

(c) Which was the sunniest month? _____

(d) How many sunny days were there in April and May altogether? _____

2. Look at the table and draw a pictogram with the information.

Type of bulb	Number planted
daffodil	15
snowdrop	8
tulip	11

Pictogram to show the number of bulbs planted in a garden	
daffodil	
snowdrop	
tulip	

Draw a pictogram to show this information. Use ◯ = 2 bulbs.

Teachers' and parents' note

Ask each student to add their symbol to a pictogram to ensure that they understand how the symbols work. Give students other opportunities to collect data and display it in pictograms using symbols representing one or two objects.

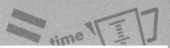

Carroll diagrams

Read it!

Key words: Carroll diagram, criteria, sort

A **Carroll diagram** is used to **sort** data such as numbers or shapes using 2 of their properties.

Properties such as even numbers or regular shapes are called **criteria**.

For example:

Example: Look at this Carroll diagram.
Question: Which shapes have the criteria:
has 4 sides   **and**   has right angles?
Answer: Square and rectangle.

	has 4 sides	does **not** have 4 sides
has right angles		
does **not** have right angles		

Language focus!

Singular	Plural
property	properties
criterion	criteria

The rows and columns of the diagram are always labelled
• has the criterion
• does **not** have the criterion.

Think about it!

Write all the numbers from 5 to 15 in the correct place on the Carroll diagram.

	even number	**not** an even number
multiple of 5		
not a multiple of 5		

Practise it!

1. Write the names of these shapes in the correct place on the Carroll diagram.

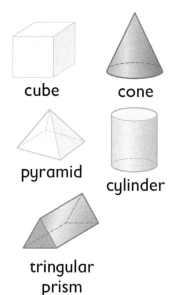

cube   cone

pyramid

cylinder

tringular
prism

	has vertices	does not have vertices
has a circular face		
does not have a circular face		

2. Look at the Carroll diagram.

Draw a ring around the numbers that are in the wrong place.

	greater than 20	not greater than 20
multiple of 2	72 18 34	6 15 10
not a multiple of 2	99 53 45	21 3 7

3. Here are four labels.

3-digit number	not a 3-digit number	odd	not odd

Write each label in the correct position on the Carroll diagram.

	135	128
	71 45	1000

Teachers' and parents' note

Discuss the criteria that may be used for sorting, such as shapes that have lines of symmetry or multiples of 10. Make sure students understand that the criteria in the rows and columns must be linked, for example use **even** and **not even** not **even** and **odd**, unlike Venn diagrams.

Venn diagrams

Read it!

Key words: criteria, set, Venn diagram

A **set** is a collection of related things, such as odd numbers, 2D shapes, fruit or wild animals.

A **Venn diagram** is used to show how one **set** is related to another.

For example:

Diagram A

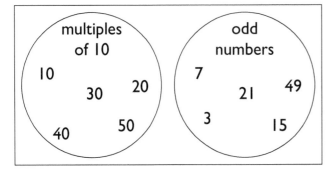

Diagram B

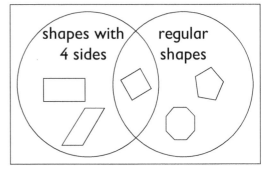

No numbers are in both sets.

The square is in both sets.

Example:
Question: What is in the set of regular shapes in diagram B?
Answer: Regular pentagon, regular octagon, square.

Language focus!

Universal set

The rectangle around the Venn diagram represents the **universal** set.

Write numbers or objects that do not belong in either set outside the circles but inside the rectangle. Look at this diagram.

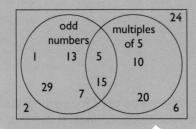

Think about it!

Draw an arrow to show the correct place for each shape in the Venn diagram.

 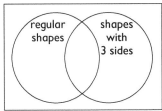 

Practise it!

1. **Write these numbers in the correct place in the Venn diagram.**

   | 25, 8, 5, 42, 30, 27, 10, 13, 6 |

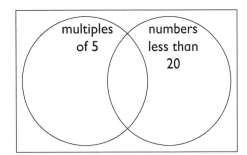

2. **Look at the Venn diagram below.**

   (a) Write 3 numbers that belong in both sets (where the circles overlap).

   —————, —————, —————

   (b) Write 3 numbers that only belong to set B.

   —————, —————, —————

   (c) Write 3 numbers that do not belong in either set.

   —————, —————, —————

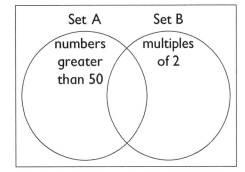

Teachers' and parents' note

Try sorting shapes practically using two hoops, a set of 2D shapes and some labels, for example shapes containing a right angle, shapes with three sides and so on. The hoops can be overlapped to show where sets intersect. This activity can be adapted to sort 3D shapes or numbers using different criteria.

Key words

Number

Unit 1 Read and write numbers to 1000
digit, place, place value, unit, ten, hundred, thousand

Unit 2 Partition numbers
partition, hundreds, tens, units

Unit 3 Order and compare numbers
compare, in between, greater than, largest, less than, order, smallest

Unit 4 Patterns and sequences
count on, count back, continue, pattern, rule, sequence

Unit 5 Rounding
round, round down, round up, round to the nearest

Unit 6 Fractions
fraction, equal part, half, third, quarter, whole

Unit 7 Equivalent fractions
equivalent, half, quarter, eighth, tenth

Unit 8 Mixed numbers
mixed number

Unit 9 Addition
add, altogether, count on, increase by, jottings, more, more than, number line, plus, sum, total

Unit 10 Subtraction
count back, decrease by, difference between, leave, less than, minus, subtract, take away

Unit 11 Addition and subtraction facts
answer, equals, missing number, number sentence, operation, represents

Unit 12 Multiplication
array, columns, group, groups of, lots of, multiply, rows, times

Unit 13 Division
divide, even, groups of, left over, odd, remainder, share equally

Unit 14 Doubles and halves
double, half, halve, inverse, opposite

Unit 15 Times tables
division, inverse, multiple, multiplication, times table

Unit 16 Word problems
answer, number sentence, operation, word problem

Geometry

Unit 17 2D shapes
circle, rectangle, semicircle, square, triangle, classify, property, edge, side, vertex, vertices

Unit 18 Regular shapes
classify, irregular, hexagon, octagon, pentagon, regular

Unit 19 Right angles
angle, right angle, turn, straight line

Unit 20 Line symmetry
line of symmetry, mirror line, reflection, symmetrical, symmetry

Unit 21 3D shapes
cone, cube, cuboid, cylinder, sphere, curved, edge, face, flat, vertices

Unit 22 Pyramids and prisms
base, edge, face, prism, pyramid, vertex

Unit 23 Nets
edge, face, net

Unit 24 Position and movement
above, below, down, left, position, right, route, up

Unit 25 Using grids
column, down, grid, left, position, right, row, up

Measures

Unit 26 Length
height, length, long, ruler, tall, wide, width, centimetres, kilometres, metres

Unit 27 Mass
balance, gram, heavy, kilogram, light, scales, weigh

Unit 28 Capacity
empty, full, litre, millilitre, contains, pours

Unit 29 Telling the time
analogue clock, digital clock, past, to, day, hour, minute, second

Unit 30 Using a calendar
calendar, date, day, month, week, year

Unit 31 Using measurements
compare, estimate, measurement, measuring jug, ruler, scales, centimetre, metre, kilometre, grams, kilograms, millilitres, litres

Data handling

Unit 32 Tally charts
frequency table, represent, tally, tally chart, total

Unit 33 Bar charts
axis, bar chart, horizontal, label, scale, title, vertical

Unit 34 Pictograms
key, list, pictogram, represents, symbol, title

Unit 35 Carroll diagrams
Carroll diagram, criteria, sort

Unit 36 Venn diagrams
criteria, set, Venn diagram

Notes